THE GREMLINS STORYBOOK

by Mary Carey

A GOLDEN BOOK • NEW YORK

Western Publishing Company, Inc., Racine Wisconsin 53404

Billy Peltzer was late!

It was 8:54 when he opened the back door of the bank. He eased himself through, let the door close, then hurried toward the tellers' windows.

"Peltzer!" said a too-familiar voice.

Billy sighed. Mr. Corben was there in the doorway of his office, and he was looking at his watch. "Seventeen minutes and thirty-three seconds late, William," he said. "What have you got to say for yourself?"

"I'm sorry Mr. Corben," Billy replied. "It won't happen again."

"See that it doesn't, William," said Mr. Corben. "Now get to work."

Mr. Corben stepped back into his office and shut the door. Billy went to his teller's window.

The bell rang. The bank was open for business, and customers streamed in. In no time a line had formed in front of the tellers.

Then Mrs. Deagle appeared. Mrs. Deagle did not tolerate lines. She ignored this one and charged through, scattering the customers. She put her elbows on the counter in front of Billy, and she glared.

"Good morning, Mrs. Deagle," said Billy.

"I want your dog," said Mrs. Deagle.

"What?" said Billy.

"Your dog!" Mrs. Deagle was shaking with rage. "He's a menace! He's been chasing my little kitties!"

"Mrs. Deagle, I'm sorry. But it's nothing personal with Barney. Any dog who sees a cat…"

"A savage beast!" cried Mrs. Deagle. "He bit my nephew Douglas!"

"Douglas was trying to burn off his tail with a propane torch. He was only trying to…"

"You give him to me!" shrieked Mrs. Deagle. "I'll have the kennel people put him to sleep. It will be painless. If I have to catch him myself, he'll really get what he deserves!"

"Mrs. Deagle, if you'll only…"

"No excuses!" snapped Mrs. Deagle. "You're just like your father, and I've listened to his excuses for years. Late with the rent, and always an excuse. A loser! And so are you!"

Mrs. Deagle turned to glare at the customers waiting in line. They cringed. Mrs. Deagle held mortgages on most of the property in Kingston Falls, including all of their homes.

"Losers! Every one of you!" she said now. "Poor, pathetic losers!"

She made for the door. The others stepped out of her way. The bank door swung open, and she was gone.

"The old troll!" said Kate Beringer. Kate was the teller at the window next to Billy's. She was about Billy's age, and she was beautiful. Billy wanted to ask her for a date, but he hadn't found the courage yet. The morning had not gone well, and he didn't feel that now was a good time to take the chance.

🎁🎁🎁🎁🎁

Billy's father was an inventor. He was not a famous inventor. He was certainly not a rich one. He was a busy inventor, however. He had developed dozens of "gizmos"—small appliances and gadgets. He was on the road a lot trying to sell these inventions.

He returned home from a business trip that evening. He had a Christmas poinsettia in a pot for Billy's mother. For Billy, he had something a little more special.

"It's your present, son," he said, "but you can't wait until Christmas. You've got to look at it now."

Mr. Peltzer watched as Billy undid the wrappings and took the lid off the box.

Billy blinked. He saw big eyes looking up at him and two arms reaching out for him. The little animal in the box had fluffy fur, big ears, a wide mouth, and paws that looked like little hands.

"Your new pet," said Mr. Peltzer. "I found him in an old shop in Chinatown."

"Great!" cried Billy. "But Dad, what is he?"

"A Mogwai," said Mr. Peltzer. "At least that's what the old Chinese man in the store called him. He's a smart little guy. He's figured out how to work most of my gizmos."

"Gizmo—that's a great name for him," said Billy. "You like that name, boy?"

The little animal giggled as if he understood. Then he climbed onto Billy's shoulder and licked his cheek.

"Oh, I've got to get a picture of that!" said Mrs. Peltzer, laughing. She ran to get her camera. She snapped the picture, the flashbulb flared, and the room was suddenly lit with bright light.

Gizmo screamed. A second later he was clinging to Mr. Peltzer and trembling.

"I should have warned you about that," said Mr. Peltzer. "Gizmo is a special little animal, and bright light hurts him. He can't go out in the sun, not ever. The old Chinese man told me sunlight could kill him. And he can never have any water. He doesn't drink water, and he doesn't bathe."

"Oh, great!" moaned Mrs. Peltzer.

Mr. Peltzer pretended not to hear. "One more thing, even more important than the water or the light is the time he gets his food," he said. "Never feed him after midnight—never!"

Billy was astonished. "Why? Does he turn into a pumpkin or something?"

"I don't know," his dad admitted. "But the old man said that to own a Mogwai is a big responsibility, so let's be careful."

Gizmo slept in Billy's room that night. After a few complaining growls, even Billy's dog, Barney, accepted him. And when Billy said good night, Gizmo's answer sounded much like, "Good night, Billy."

A talented pet! He could even mimic human speech!

The next morning Billy tried to tell Kate about the Mogwai. She listened, but she didn't seem terribly interested, and Billy soon learned why.

"I heard Mrs. Deagle talking to Mr. Corben," said Kate. "She's going to foreclose the mortgages and take away the property of all the people who owe her money. That means half the people in town!"

Billy's heart gave a great thump. His father owed Mrs. Deagle money. "But she can't take everything!" Billy protested. "What would she do with all those houses?"

"She doesn't care about the houses. She wants the land. The people from Hi-Tox Chemical want to build a plant here in Kingston Falls; she'll sell the land to Hi-Tox."

"Hi-Tox? But that would wreck the town!"

"She doesn't care," said Kate. "It's just a big game to her. Billy, we've got to stop her."

Billy agreed, but couldn't think of how. He was still puzzling about it that evening as he stood in the kitchen and tried to get the Peltzer Peeler-Juicer to work.

The Peeler-Juicer was one of Mr. Peltzer's simpler inventions, but that didn't mean it was reliable. This evening it chopped Billy's orange to pulp. Then it sprayed juice and pulp all over the walls and wouldn't turn off.

Billy unplugged the machine. When his friend Pete Fountaine came over five minutes later, Billy had salvaged half a glass of juice and cleaned the walls a bit.

"You ought to buy your juice in a carton," said Pete. "It's easier."

"Yeah," said Billy.

Pete was eleven, and he liked visiting Billy. Billy never made Pete feel like a little kid just because he was older and taller.

"C'mon up to my room," Billy said. "I've got something to show you."

When Billy and Pete came into Billy's attic room carrying the orange juice and a plate of brownies, they found Gizmo watching television.

"Hey, neat!" cried Pete. "Where'd you get him? And what is he, anyhow?"

"My dad brought him back from his trip. I don't know exactly what he is. My dad says his last owner called him a Mogwai. We call him Gizmo."

Gizmo smelled the chocolate brownies. He scampered to the desk and took one.

Pete was fascinated by Gizmo. As he reached to pick Gizmo up, he knocked over a glass of water. Water spilled out and washed over the desk.

Suddenly Gizmo screamed! It was a horrible scream—high pitched and tortured.

"Oh, gosh!" yelled Pete.

Gizmo's back arched. He twisted with pain and shrieked again. Big ugly blisters rose on his body, everywhere that the water had touched him.

Billy and Pete heard a nasty little popping sound, and one of the blisters burst. A small, fuzzy ball shot out and landed on the desk. It rolled an inch or two, then uncurled and grew bigger—and there stood another Mogwai!

Pete gulped and clutched at Billy.

A second blister burst, and a second fuzzy ball dropped from Gizmo's side. Then there was a third burst, and a fourth. The little balls wriggled and moved. There was a final pop and the spots on Gizmo's body faded and disappeared. The Mogwai was whole and well again. It might all have been a weird dream except that now there were five new creatures on the desk. Five like Gizmo.

But not exactly like Gizmo. The new Mogwais were lighter in color, and they had a sly look that made Billy uneasy. There was one with a jagged white stripe, and he looked almost vicious.

"I don't get it," said Pete. "What happened?"

"The water," said Billy. "The old Chinese man said the Mogwai should never have water. I wonder if it's only water that does it, or if anything wet would make them multiply." Billy experimented. He splashed a few drops of orange juice on one of the Mogwai. Nothing happened. He just licked the drops off his skin, and seemed to enjoy the taste.

"It's only water that does it," Billy decided.

Mr. Peltzer was making some changes on his new gadget, the Peltzer Bathroom Buddy, when Billy came into the workshop.

"Look at this," said Mr. Peltzer to Billy. "Suppose you're on a trip someplace and you have to see an important client. Suddenly you remember that you forgot to shave."

He touched a button on the side of the Bathroom Buddy. A tiny razor popped out of the thing.

"Hey, that's pretty neat!" said Billy. He looked at the gadget more closely, and he saw a second new button on it. It was not the button that controlled the pop-up toothbrush or the self-squeezing toothpaste or the disposable face towel. Billy pressed the button to see what would happen.

A burst of shaving cream spurted out and splattered all over Mr. Peltzer's face.

"If you're going to shave," said Mr. Peltzer patiently, "you'll need shaving cream."

"Right!" said Billy. "Shaving cream."

"I have to figure out how to lower the pressure on it," said Mr. Peltzer. "Otherwise it works perfectly."

That night the five new Mogwai beckoned Barney outside. Suddenly many little hands clutched at him. Something tangled itself around him, and he was lifted off his feet.

It was the middle of the night when Billy heard whimpering. He stumbled down the stairs in his pajamas and opened the front door.

Barney was there, hanging from the roof, helpless in a tangle of Christmas lights. He was wheezing and coughing and shivering. Billy got him down and carried him into the kitchen. He sat down and tried to massage some life back into Barney.

Billy was still there in the morning when his father came down with his suitcase. Billy was more angry than he had ever been. "It was Mrs. Deagle!" he announced to his parents. "She's been threatening to get Barney!"

"Billy, we can't prove that," said Mrs. Peltzer. "Listen, let Dad take Barney with him today. He can drop him off at Grandma's on his way to the inventors' convention. That will keep Barney out of Mrs. Deagle's way for a couple of days."

Billy looked doubtful. He and Barney had never been separated before. But at last he agreed. His mother's idea made sense.

At work that day, Billy brooded about Mrs. Deagle—and about the Mogwais he had left in his room. He had to know more about the little creatures!

When the bank closed that afternoon he hurried home and put one of the Mogwais into a shoe box. Billy brought the creature to his former science teacher, Mr. Hanson, at the Kingston Avenue School.

"Well, Billy! What brings you back here?" asked Mr. Hanson.

"I've got something I want to show you," said Billy.

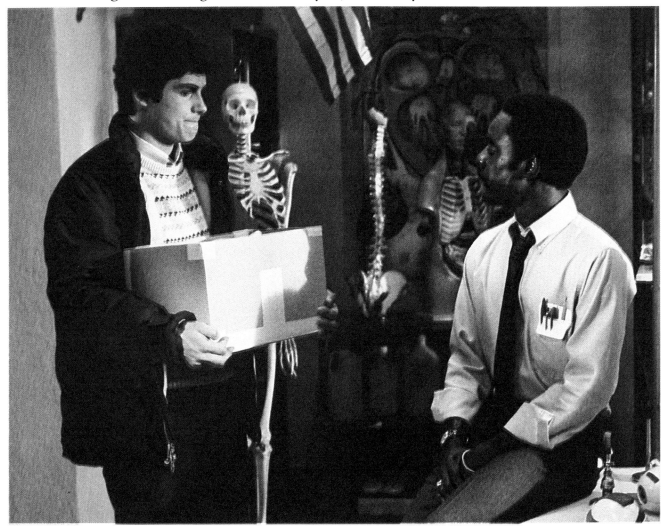

Billy drew the blinds and switched off the lights. Then he opened his shoe box and took out a cuddly, big-eyed Mogwai.

Mr. Hanson was bewildered. "What is it?" he asked.

"It's called a Mogwai," replied Billy. "I want you to see what happens when water touches him." Billy took a dropper and applied a single drop of water to the Mogwai's skin.

The little animal screamed, and Mr. Hanson jumped.

A blister formed on the Mogwai's side. It grew and burst.

The fuzzy brown ball dropped to the lab table, uncurled, and became a second Mogwai.

"Good night!" cried Mr. Hanson.

"You said it exactly," agreed Billy.

Mr. Hanson shook his head. "Can you leave one here overnight? I'd like to run some tests."

"I was hoping you'd say that," Billy replied. He put one of the Mogwai back into the shoe box. The second creature let out a scream.

"I guess they don't like to be separated," said Mr. Hanson. "Sorry, little guy." Mr. Hanson put the second Mogwai into a hamster cage and Billy went on his way.

That night Billy went to Dorry's Pub, a popular local night spot.

Mrs. Deagle was planning to take over Dorry's Pub, close it up, and sell it to Hi-Tox. Kate and Billy and some of their friends had decided that this wouldn't happen. They had formed a volunteer corps of waitresses and waiters. They would work without pay for Dorry, so he could use that money to pay off Mrs. Deagle. This evening Kate was working as a waitress.

Billy liked the evenings at Dorry's, and he liked walking Kate home after the pub closed. On this particular night Billy got up his courage at last, and he asked Kate for a date.

"I'd love it!" said Kate.

Billy was surprised and delighted, and he hurried home in a happy daze. When he got home, Billy found the Mogwais with their arms outstretched, begging for food. He glanced at his clock. "It's only 11:40," Billy thought. "I guess it's still O.K. to feed them." He went to the kitchen, got a plate of leftover fried chicken from the refrigerator, and took it up to them.

Gizmo would not eat any chicken. He perched on the bookcase and watched the others eat, and he whined. He seemed to be saying, "No, no, no!" in his high little voice.

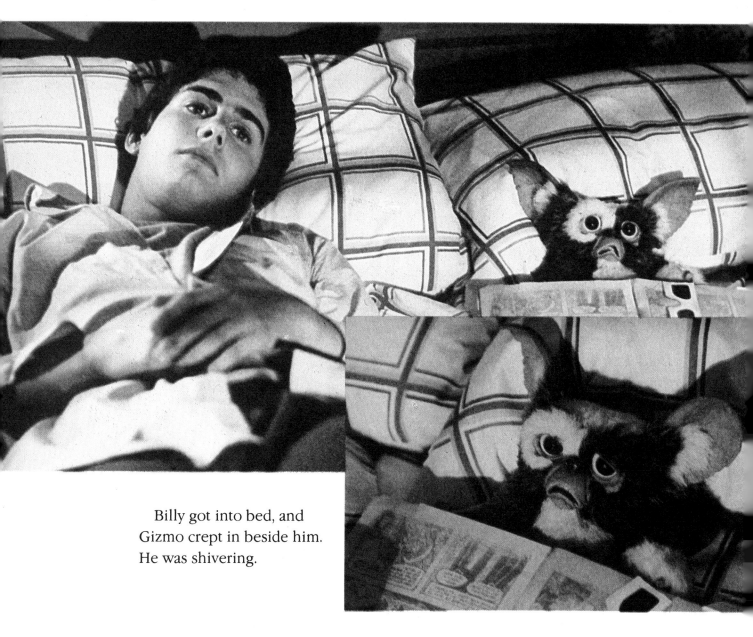

Billy got into bed, and Gizmo crept in beside him. He was shivering.

In the morning Billy woke and looked for the Mogwais. They should have been sleeping in the open trunk near the bed, but they weren't. They weren't scampering on the floor either, or playing with the pens on the desk. Instead of small furry animals, Billy saw pods on the floor—things that looked like big cocoons. They were covered with some nasty, sticky stuff.

Gizmo saw them and whimpered.

"What is it, Gizmo?" whispered Billy. "What's going on?"

Then Billy remembered the chicken. "I'm sure I fed them before midnight," said Billy. "The clock said 11:40." Billy looked at his clock. It *still* read 11:40 pm! Billy checked the power cord, and saw that it had been chewed through—by the Mogwais, no doubt. "Oh no!" he said. "I must have fed them after midnight!"

🎁 🎁 🎁 🎁 🎁

After work, Billy went back to the school. Mr. Hanson was in his classroom with one ruined hamster cage and one sticky pod. The pod had broken the wires of the cage.

"It's in the pupal stage," said Mr. Hanson, "like a butterfly. That means your Mogwai is changing to another form."

Billy frowned. "But why did *this* one spin a cocoon?"

Mr. Hanson looked startled—and guilty. "I left part of a sandwich on the lab table last night," he admitted. "It was gone this morning."

"So this one ate after midnight, too!" said Billy.

"Looks like it," agreed Mr. Hanson. "Interesting creature. I did a blood test on it. It can only multiply with water if the environmental temperature is over 30 degrees. We don't know much more about these little guys."

Billy nodded. "We'll know more when the cocoons hatch." He went home to watch his cocoons.

Nothing happened until two days before Christmas. Mr. Hanson called the bank, and he was breathless with excitement. "Billy, it just hatched!"

"What's it look like?" Billy asked.

"I don't know yet. It's hiding under the lab table. Come on over!"

Billy was out the door without even trying to explain to Mr. Corben, and he ran all the way to the school.

Classes were over for the day, but the side door was still open. Billy raced up the stairs to the science room.

At first he thought the room was empty. But then he saw Mr. Hanson. The teacher was stretched out on the floor near the bookshelves.

Billy knelt and touched the teacher's hand. He had known the instant he saw him. Roy Hanson was dead. A giant model of the human brain had fallen from a bookcase, and landed right on top of him.

Billy stood up. He had to call the police, or a doctor, or somebody.

Just then, something moved in the shadows beyond the desk. There was an eraser on the floor, and it had a chunk taken out of it as if something had bitten it.

Billy bent to pick up the eraser. There was a flash of movement—a quick, brutal strike from the shadows.

Billy jumped back. Pain shot up his arm and he saw blood. The thing had clawed him.

The first aid room was open. Billy found bandages in the first cupboard on the far wall. He wrapped the bandages around his arm, then looked for adhesive tape. He started to open the second cupboard.

There was a snarl. Billy had a quick, horrifying glimpse of needle-sharp teeth in a wide mouth. He saw scales instead of fur, claws instead of pudgy hands.

The claws slashed out. Billy fell back and saw the creature bolt out the door with incredible speed.

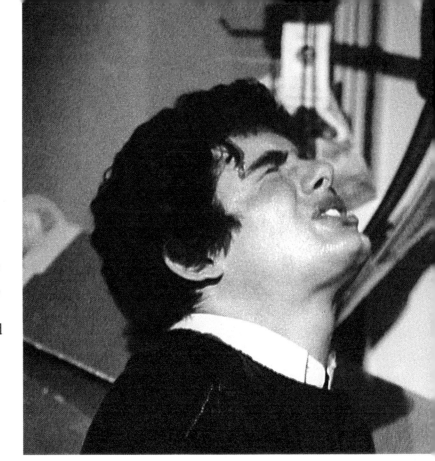

Then Billy remembered the pods at home. Five of them. And his mother was there alone!

Billy raced down the stairs and out the door. He was sweating when he put his dime in the slot of the pay phone and dialed his home number.

"Please answer, Mom!" he breathed. "Please!"

She did.

"Mom, get out of the house quick! They hatched!"

"Billy, what's the matter?"

"Run, Mom. They've already killed Mr. Hanson!"

"The science teacher? He was so nice."

"Yes he was, Mom. Don't just stand there. Go quick, before . . . "

The line went dead.

"Mom?" yelled Billy. "Mom!"

He dropped the telephone and ran.

Later he would never remember anything about that desperate sprint home. He remembered only slamming in through his own front door and snatching the sword that hung on the wall near the stairs. Then he heard a terrible giggle.

The living room was in chaos, with broken china everywhere. Christmas stockings were scattered on the floor. The Christmas tree had fallen. His mother was under it. She was choking.

Billy threw the tree aside. His mother's face was ghastly white. The creature was on top of her. It was trying to get those terrible teeth into her neck!

Billy's sword flashed up and down. The blade severed the creature's head from its body.

Again there was a giggle. Another little beast sat on the windowsill. Billy recognized it. It was the one that Billy had begun to call "Stripe"—since he had that jagged white stripe running down his back.

He hissed at Billy, then smashed out through the window and was gone.

"Billy!" cried Mrs. Peltzer. She sat up, shaking. "Thank God!"

He got her into a chair and brought water
from the kitchen. There was something nasty in
the Peeler-Juicer. He realized that the greenish
pulp there must have been one of the little
beasts. Something else was baked to a crisp in
the microwave oven. That would account for a
second beast. He had beheaded one, and there
was one in the china cabinet, stabbed with
scissors. Four.

Stripe and the one from the school were the
only survivors. He had to stop them. They were
killers.

He brought his mother to a neighbor's house,
and then he raced back home. He had to find
Gizmo.

He shouted, but got no answer. The attic
room was empty except for broken, husklike
remains of the pods. There was a smear of
blood on the bureau and spatters of red on the
broken glass of a framed photograph.

"Gizmo!" Billy wept. "Gizmo, they killed
you!"

Then he heard a tiny voice calling. It sounded as if it was calling his name. Yet it wasn't a human voice. It was Gizmo, calling from the basement. He had escaped down the laundry chute.

Billy ran down the stairs. The heap of clothing on the floor under the chute moved when he called, and Gizmo popped out from under the towels and shirts.

Billy grinned. Except for a few scrapes, Gizmo was unharmed.

"Gizmo, you're okay!" cried Billy.

Gizmo made a noise as if to say, "You bet."

"Fine," said Billy. "So let's go get 'em!"

Billy tucked the Mogwai into his backpack and set out.

From that moment on, Billy thought of the little beasts as gremlins. Funny old Mr. Futterman, his neighbor, always said it was gremlins who made things go wrong. Billy didn't believe in Mr. Futterman's gremlins, but he did believe in the ones he had just seen.

He found the tiny footprints in the snow under the living room window. They went off down the street toward the woods at the end of the block. Billy followed them with a flashlight in hand, for it was dark now. The footprints went on through the woods and out the far side.

The footprints led to the YMCA. They went to the side of the building, where Billy found a broken window.

The front door was unlocked, and he let himself into a long corridor. At the end of the corridor Billy felt for a light switch, but there was none. He clicked his flashlight on and swept it back and forth. He saw bleachers, and a metal box—an electrical box that had to contain light switches.

He knew what to do. Turn on every light in the place! That would fix Stripe.

He went to the box and flipped up the lid.

The beast leaped. It had waited in the box, and now it fastened to him, its claws digging into his chest. Billy spun, falling, trying to fight Stripe off. He hit the floor and the jolt knocked Gizmo out of the backpack. The flashlight bounced away.

Suddenly Billy was blinking and Stripe was screaming.

Gizmo had the flashlight. He was holding it so that the beam shone away from himself and straight at Stripe.

Stripe cowered back—and then dropped out of sight.

Billy heard a splash.

The pool! Stripe had fallen into the swimming pool.

A rumble came from the water. Billy saw bubbles and ripples. The rumble grew louder.

The creature was multiplying. Down at the bottom of the pool, where they couldn't get at it, it was producing more gremlins!

Billy grabbed Gizmo and ran!

Billy's neighbor, Mr. Futterman, was trying to watch his television. He was not having much luck. The screen kept filling with snow.

Mr. Futterman mumbled and grumbled. At last he stamped out into the night to check his antenna.

He was not in time to see the gremlins swinging from the antenna. He *was* in time to hear his snow plow start with a roar. It came crashing out through the garage door.

Mr. Futterman shrieked. He couldn't believe it. His very own snow plow was rumbling straight toward him!

Mrs. Futterman came to the glass door at the back of the house. She saw Mr. Futterman running from the plow, and she opened the door. "Quick," she cried. "In here!"

Mr. Futterman zipped into the house.

The snow plow climbed the back steps after him.

Mr. and Mrs. Futterman raced into the living room. Then, as Mrs. Futterman screamed and screamed, the plow came crashing through the walls.

Nasty old Mrs. Deagle was feeding her cats. There were nine of them, and they stood in a circle to watch her put the cat food into the nine separate bowls. When she finished, they began to eat. She watched them, not noticing the sudden gust of cold air around her ankles. Something had come into the house through the cat door.

Mrs. Deagle *did* notice the children who were out on the lawn singing Christmas carols. Mrs. Deagle hated Christmas carols. She stamped to the front door and threw it open.

"Go away!" cried Mrs. Deagle. "Get off my lawn!"

The children stopped singing. They straggled away and Mrs. Deagle closed her door.

She made for the electric stair climber that had been installed beside her bannister. But the sound of caroling came again from the lawn. This time it was higher in pitch and the words were not clear. It was more a hum than a song. But she was sure it was the children.

Mrs. Deagle went to the door again, and flung it wide. "I told you brats to get off my…"

She stopped.

There were no children. Instead, six gremlins grinned at Mrs. Deagle from the bottom of the porch steps. Mrs. Deagle saw dancing, wicked eyes and pointed, needle-like teeth.

She screamed and slammed the door.

What were those things? She'd call the police! But first she'd get upstairs, away from the ugly little creatures—far away!

She staggered to the stair climber and sat down. Her shaking finger touched the button marked "Up."

The chair whizzed up suddenly, a hundred times faster than it had ever moved before. It shot along the bannister.

At the top of the stairs the chair shot off its track. It flew across the landing and crashed through the window. Mrs. Deagle plummeted to the ground.

The gremlin on the landing looked out through the shattered window, and giggled.

🎁 🎁 🎁 🎁 🎁

At first Billy ran to the sheriff's office. There was no one there. Then he thought of Kate. She would be at Dorry's by now.

Billy ran home to get his car. He dashed through the snowy streets, and as he passed Mr. Futterman's house he heard an uproar. He did not stop until he reached his car. He yanked open the door and piled in.

The drive downtown was a nightmare. Billy saw ruin and destruction everywhere. Cars blocked intersections, and windows were smashed. At Maple and Third a man struggled with a letter box. Something inside the box had reached out to grab him. He broke free at last and ran.

The movie theater looked blank and deserted. So did the bank. At first Billy thought that Dorry's was deserted too.

Kate was inside the pub. When she saw headlights on the street she almost sobbed. The pub was alive with ugly, clawing, grinning gremlins. Dorry's regular patrons had fled when the gremlins invaded the place, smashing the windows, upsetting the tables, pounding on the bar. Kate didn't know where Dorry was now. She didn't know where anyone was. She was alone with the gremlins and they were squealing for drinks. One of them had passed out on top of the bar.

Now there were headlights on the street. Help was coming. She knew that the creatures were afraid of light. She had seen one playing with a lighter; when it flamed up, the gremlin had been frightened.

Kate glanced behind her. Dorry kept a camera with a flash attachment on the shelf above the back bar. Kate seized it and pointed it at the gremlins. She snapped the shutter and the flash flared.

The gremlins screeched and scattered, and Kate ran for the window.

The car swerved toward the pub. The headlights filled the window. They were bright, blinding.

Gremlins screamed and ran to shelter in whatever shadow they could find. Kate scrambled through the window and ran toward the blessed, beautiful light. Then she saw Billy—in his crazy old car. She jumped in just as bottles and ash trays started flying from the pub.

Then, at the worst of moments, the car died. It wouldn't start again, and something next to Kate squealed.

Kate screamed.

"It's okay! It's okay!" cried Billy. "That's Gizmo!"

Kate saw Billy stow the furry little animal in his backpack. "A phone!" said Billy. "We've got to get to a phone and call the Army—or the National Guard—or somebody!"

Next to Dorry's, the bank door was open. Kate and Billy ran for it, ducking low to avoid the flying bottles. But the telephone on the counter inside the bank was dead.

"They thought of everything, didn't they?" said Billy bitterly.

Kate nodded, and she looked toward the street. Suddenly it was quiet. The squealing from Dorry's had stopped.

"Are they gone?" asked Kate.

Dorry's was silent and empty, and nothing moved on the street. Gizmo made one of his urgent little Mogwai noises and pointed across the square to the theater.

Billy saw the little footprints in the snow. They went toward the theater, and Billy understood. Soon it would be light. The gremlins had to hide from the light, and what better place than a dark movie theater? They were probably all there together. Mr. Hanson had said they didn't like to be separated.

"This is our chance," said Billy. "Now we can get them!"

"Swell," said Kate. "How do we do that?"

"First we make sure they're in there. Then we blow the place up."

They crossed the square and tiptoed into the theater lobby. They peeked into the auditorium and saw images flickering on the screen. The gremlins were watching a movie. They were also gobbling candy and popcorn.

Kate and Billy stole out and down an alley to the back door of the theater. It opened to a cluttered area behind the screen where a trap door led to the basement.

They both went down, and Billy turned on every gas jet he could find in the boiler room.

"Let's go!" he whispered as gas hissed into the room.

Kate scooted up and out through the trap door. Billy came after her with Gizmo in his backpack. He had a piece of rag he had found on the floor, and as he eased the trap door down he slipped the rag between the door and the floor. Then he touched a match to the rag.

It was oily, and it burned nicely. Billy and Kate ran out into the cool, fresh night.

They were safely across the street when the theater blew. There was a muffled boom at first. The doors blew off and the roof shook. The theater filled with flames, the gremlins screamed. They were all destroyed.

It was over. Billy and Kate had won!

Suddenly Gizmo squealed and pointed.

A lone gremlin stood in front of Montgomery Ward. It was Stripe, and he had an armful of candy.

Billy knew what must have happened. When the candy in the theater lobby was all gone, Stripe had run across the street to help himself to the goodies at Montgomery Ward.

Gizmo growled at Stripe, and the gremlin dropped his candy and fled back into the dark department store.

Billy and Kate went after him. Once they were inside, Kate took Gizmo and went to find the light switches. Billy stalked the shadowy aisles, listening for the sound of small feet scampering.

Out of nowhere came a buzzing.

Billy jumped.

Metallic footsteps clicked across the floor. Then Billy heard the terrible gremlin giggle. Stripe had sent a toy robot marching across the aisle.

A toy truck rolled behind the robot. Behind the truck a tin duck waddled and quacked.

Billy peeped over the counter top. Stripe was sitting on the floor behind the counter, winding up toys.

Billy charged!

A wind-up bird whirred straight into his face. He stumbled back and fell, and the gremlin fled.

Billy got to his feet and listened. He heard the gremlin move somewhere to his right. Billy swung toward the noise.

Stripe had a bow and arrow, and the bow was drawn taut. The arrow was aimed right at Billy, and before Billy could move, there was a twang. The arrow struck Billy's arm.

Then the lights went on.

The glare was blinding agony to Stripe. He screeched and bounded off to find a dark place.

Billy looked up. He saw Kate and Gizmo in the glass-enclosed electrical booth on the second floor, and he shouted. "More lights!" he yelled. "Turn on everything!"

Kate did. She flipped every switch in front of her.

More lights came on. The store was flooded with brilliance. Music came on too. Recorded announcements boomed over the public address system.

Unfortunately, something else came on. In the store's greenhouse section, a fountain sent a spray of water high into the air.

Stripe heard the water, and he ran for it.

"Kate, the fountain!" shouted Billy. "Turn off the fountain!"

She tried, but she didn't know which switch controlled the fountain. She had turned on so many things! Frantically she flipped switches, and lights died one by one.

Billy chased after the gremlin.

He arrived too late. Stripe was in the fountain. He danced under the spray of water, and blisters began to form on his skin.

It was then that Mr. Peltzer and Barney arrived. Mr. Peltzer had tried to telephone home, but all the lines were dead. He drove back to Kingston Falls. The smoke from the exploding theater drew him downtown. It was Barney who led him into Montgomery Ward. They showed up just in time to see Stripe splashing around in the fountain.

Meanwhile, a little toy car came speeding down the aisle with Gizmo at the wheel. He zipped around the corner on two wheels and crashed into the wall. The bubbles on Stripe's hide had swelled and grown. Any second they would burst, and hordes of gremlins would swarm out of the fountain!

Gizmo looked up. Overhead a canvas tarp covered a skylight. A glint of daylight showed at the edge of the tarp, which was held in place by a rope that came down the wall and was tied to a metal bar.

Gizmo had to stand on a flower pot to reach the rope. He tugged at the knot, and for a moment nothing gave. But at last the knot came loose. The rope snapped free and the tarp unpeeled from the skylight.

Sunlight flooded the room. Stripe screamed. The bubbles on his skin withered and dried and vanished. Steam rose in a cloud. Stripe was gone; there remained only a skeleton, and then the skeleton fell and shattered into a million pieces.

The struggle was over. The last gremlin was dead.

Reporters and television crews poured into the town. On Christmas Day there was almost nothing on television but the story of the gremlins. The set was on in the Peltzer living room, and the Peltzers watched. Even though they knew the story too well, they found a fascination in it.

Even Gizmo kept his eyes on the picture tube. The little creature lay on the sofa with Mr. Peltzer's muffler spread over him to keep him warm. He was hurt, but not badly. Billy's injuries were minor, as well.

The doorbell rang, and Mr. Peltzer went to answer it. He expected to see a newsman. Instead he saw the old Chinese shopkeeper who had once owned Gizmo.

Gizmo sat up even before he saw the man, and he began to hum. When the visitor came into the living room, Gizmo held out his arms. The old man picked Gizmo up and held him.

It was over. Billy knew it. Gizmo was going home, and Billy would not move a muscle to stop him. Not when Gizmo was so happy.

"I warn you that Mogwai is special animal," said the Chinese man to Mr. Peltzer. "To have Mogwai means much responsibility."

Billy glanced at the TV screen. He saw the ruins of Kingston Falls. What the old man said was true.

"Chinese philosopher once write, 'Society without responsibility is society without hope,'" said the old man. He started for the door.

"Take care of yourself, Gizmo," said Billy softly. "I'll miss you."

The Mogwai said something that was not merely a Mogwai noise. It was a name: "Billy."

Then Gizmo and the old man were gone. Billy was sure that he could hear the small creature singing as they went.